# BIRDS, BEASTS AND THE THIRD THING

# BIRDS, BEASTS AND

## INTRODUCTION BY DONALD HALL

*Julia MacRae Books*

A DIVISION OF FRANKLIN WATTS

# THE THIRD THING

Poems by

## D. H. LAWRENCE

Selected and Illustrated by

## Alice and Martin Provensen

TO THE STUDENTS

OF THE BEAUVALE BOARD SCHOOL,

EASTWOOD, NOTTINGHAMSHIRE

A. & M. P.

Text by D. H. Lawrence from *The Complete Poems of D. H. Lawrence.*
Copyright © 1964, 1971 by Angelo Ravagli and C. M. Weekley,
Executors of the Estate of Frieda Lawrence Ravagli.
Illustrations Copyright © 1982 by Alice and Martin Provensen
Introduction Copyright © 1982 by Donald Hall
First published in 1982 by The Viking Press, New York.
First published in Great Britain 1982 by Julia MacRae Books,
A Division of Franklin Watts, 8 Cork Street, London W1X 2HA
Printed in U.S.A.

British Library Cataloguing in Publication Data
Lawrence, D. H.
Birds, beasts and the third thing.
I. Title    II. Provensen, Alice
III. Provensen, Martin
821′.912    PR6023.A93
ISBN 0-86203-071-4

David Herbert Lawrence was born in a coal mining town in the English county of Nottingham in 1885. His mother had been a schoolteacher; his father hacked at the coal-face underground. He was a delicate child, not expected to survive infancy, and grew up unable to take part in games with other children at school. Instead, he walked in the countryside beyond his colliery village, along roads and footpaths heading toward Sherwood Forest, where in the old times Robin Hood and his merry men tricked the sheriff of Nottingham. He turned his back on industrialism, even as a child, and entered the natural world of horses and wild flowers — always aware, as he walked over the surface of England's green and pleasant land, that his father toiled in darkness hundreds of feet below.

When he was thirteen, the boy won a scholarship to Nottingham High School, then worked as a clerk and elementary schoolteacher before attending Nottingham University. He started to write stories and poems early, publishing in the *English Review* in 1909. Until he died of tuberculosis at forty-four, he wrote prolifically, recognized most as novelist (*Sons and Lovers, The Rainbow, Women in Love, Lady Chatterley's Lover,* etc.) and short story writer, also as an essayist, critic, and writer of travel books.

Best of all — some readers think — he wrote almost a thousand pages of poetry. At first his poems were formal and conventional, then with greater freedom and rashness and even abandon he recorded in verse his most cherished ideas and feelings to embody the natural world. For Lawrence, poems could be brief explosions of feeling, they could be witty summaries of ideas, they could be long meditations, and they were often a rapid, intense note-taking on the sensations of being alive.

Opposed to modern society with its technology and its greed, he praised the "Delight of Being Alone." Writing of flowers, or of the "Humming-Bird," he recorded his identification with the natural world and his moral judgment on contemporary human society. He loved solitude and used it as a place of vantage: "I like people quite well/ at a little distance.../ especially if I see their aloneness alive in them." In his own "aloneness" he preserved throughout his life a child's sudden vistas of revelation. He saw in "The White Horse" a vision forever lucid and shining:

> *The youth walks up to the white horse, to put its halter on*
> *and the horse looks at him in silence.*
> *They are so silent, they are in another world.*

This other world is the third thing. From an early age Lawrence showed a religious, almost mystical sense of another world, a sense of immanence which children cherish and most adults lose: "...but there is also a third thing, that makes it water/ and nobody knows what it is." Only the things that nobody knows are worth knowing.

In this book Alice and Martin Provensen have chosen verses by D. H. Lawrence suited for younger readers. With affectionate, meticulous, handsome illustrations, they have made a book that brings to beginning readers or listeners first acquaintance with a great writer they can enjoy for the rest of their lives.

DONALD HALL

# BIRDS, BEASTS AND THE THIRD THING

PEOPLE

I like people quite well
at a little distance.
I like to see them passing and passing
and going their own way,
especially if I see their aloneness alive in them.

Yet I don't want them to come near.

If they will only leave me alone

I can still have the illusion that there is room enough in the world.

*MANY MANSIONS*   When a bird flips his tail in getting his balance on a tree
he feels much gayer than if somebody had left him a fortune
or than if he'd just built himself a nest with a bathroom—
Why can't people be gay like that?

## THE MOSQUITO KNOWS

The mosquito knows full well, small as he is
he's a beast of prey.
But after all
he only takes his bellyful,
he doesn't put my blood in the bank.

*A LIVING*

A man should never earn his living,
if he earns his life he'll be lovely.

A bird
picks up its seeds or little snails
between heedless earth and heaven
in heedlessness.

But, the plucky little sport, it gives to life
song, and chirruping, gay feathers, fluff-shadowed warmth
and all the unspeakable charm of birds hopping and fluttering and being birds.
— And we, we get it all from them for nothing.

*DELIGHT OF BEING ALONE*

I know no greater delight than the sheer delight of being alone.
It makes me realise the delicious pleasure of the moon
that she has in travelling by herself: throughout time,
or the splendid growing of an ash-tree
alone, on a hill-side in the north, humming in the wind.

*RELATIVITY*

I like relativity and quantum theories
because I don't understand them
and they make me feel as if space shifted about like a swan that can't settle,
refusing to sit still and be measured;
and as if the atom were an impulsive thing
always changing its mind.

## HUMMING-BIRD

I can imagine in some otherworld
Primeval-dumb, far back
In that most awful stillness, that only gasped and hummed,
Humming-birds raced down the avenues.

Before anything had a soul,
While life was a heave of Matter, half inanimate,
This little bit chipped off in brilliance
And went whizzing through the slow, vast, succulent stems.

I believe there were no flowers then,
In the world where the humming-bird flashed ahead of creation.
I believe he pierced the slow vegetable veins with his long beak.

Probably he was big
As mosses, and little lizards, they say, were once big.
Probably he was a jabbing, terrifying monster.

We look at him through the wrong end of the long telescope of Time,
Luckily for us.

*THE THIRD THING*     Water is H$_2$O, hydrogen two parts, oxygen one, but there is also a third thing, that makes it water and nobody knows what that is.

The atom locks up two energies
but it is the third thing present that makes it an atom.

### THE RAINBOW

Even the rainbow has a body
made of the drizzling rain
and is an architecture of glistening atoms
built up, built up
yet you can't lay your hand on it,
nay, nor even your mind.

SUNSET    There is a band of dull gold in the west, and say what you like
          again and again some god of evening leans out of it
          and shares being with me, silkily
          all of twilight.

*LITTLE FISH*

The tiny fish enjoy themselves
in the sea.
Quick little splinters of life,
their little lives are fun to them
in the sea.

*SEA-WEED*

Sea-weed sways and sways and swirls
as if swaying were its form of stillness;
and if it flushes against fierce rock
it slips over it as shadows do, without hurting itself.

*SPRAY*

It is a wonder foam is so beautiful.

A wave bursts in anger on a rock, broken up

in wild white sibilant spray

and falls back, drawing in its breath with rage,

and frustration how beautiful!

*SALT*

Salt is scorched water that the sun has scorched
into substance and flaky whiteness
in the eternal opposition
between the two great ones, Fire, and the Wet.

*ELEPHANTS PLODDING*

Plod! Plod!
And what ages of time
the worn arches of their spines support!

*ELEPHANTS IN THE CIRCUS*

Elephants in the circus
have aeons of weariness round their eyes.
Yet they sit up
and show vast bellies to the children.

## SONG

Up in the high
    Swinging cherry-tree
Like a bird am I
    Clinging merrily.

Leaves whisper and titter
    As the wind races south;
And the red fruits glitter
    Cool on my mouth.

Sallies of swinging fruit
    Cold on my cheek
Swaying I snatch, and loot
    Beauties so sleek.

Scarlet and cherry red,
    Insolent gold,
Down the dark bough have fled
    Out of my hold.

Who is it singing
    Down there below?
When Red rain goes flinging—
    Hark—her quick "Oh!"

See her laugh up at me
    Through wind-snatched hair
Now see her turn to flee:
    "Oh, if you dare!"

*SPACE*　　　　　Space, of course, is alive
　　　　　　　　that's why it moves about;
　　　　　　　　and that's what makes it eternally spacious and unstuffy.

And somewhere it has a wild heart
that sends pulses even through me;
and I call it the sun;
and I feel aristocratic, noble, when I feel a pulse go through me
from the wild heart of space, that I call the sun of suns.

*TALK*

I wish people, when you sit near them,
wouldn't think it necessary to make conversation
and send thin draughts of words
blowing down your neck and your ears
and giving you a cold in your inside.

### MAN'S IMAGE

What a pity, when a man looks at himself in a glass
he doesn't bark at himself, like a dog does,
or fluff up in indignant fury, like a cat.

What a pity he sees himself so wonderful,
a little lower than the angels!
and so interesting!

*THE WHITE HORSE*

The youth walks up to the white horse, to put its halter on
and the horse looks at him in silence.
They are so silent, they are in another world.

*GREEN*

The dawn was apple-green,
    The sky was green wine held up in the sun,
The moon was a golden petal between.

She opened her eyes, and green
    They shone, clear like flowers undone
For the first time, now for the first time seen.

*ROSES*      Nature responds so beautifully.

Roses are only once-wild roses, that were given an extra chance,

So they bloomed out and filled themselves with coloured fulness

Out of sheer desire to be splendid, and more splendid.

The paintings for

BIRDS, BEASTS AND THE THIRD THING

were prepared in acrylic and pen on paper.
The art was then camera separated and printed in four
colours. The text type is 16 point Perpetua, and
the display type is hand lettered by
the artists.